15

Dedicated to Bee

Hi everyone,

I thought I would write you a book
So you could take a really good look
At what feelings truly do mean.

It is an A-Z dictionary of all the emotions
And a little story, so no commotion
To understand better what you have seen.

I'm lucky, my Mom and Dad are really great
They taught me not to hit or hate
So on them, I usually do lean.

I hope you enjoy reading my story
About all my true feelings, not my glory
I wrote truthfully about how and where I have been.

Be brave, be happy, be calm, be energetic
But also look at the feelings that are pathetic
I assure you from that, you will never be mean.

If everyone would just take time to think
About feelings, so to their heart they would link
The whole world would be loving, kind and clean.

Love,
Onionhead®

®1997

Table of Contents

Table of Contents

ACCEPTED
light feeling

to be recognized, to be believed, to be approved of

REJECTED
heavy feeling

to be refused, to be denied, to be discarded

My family went on vacation to the beach.
I tried to swim but the ocean was out of my reach.
I fell so badly and cut myself under my eye.

I was lying there rejected in the sand
As the beach goers screamed and ran,
Because it seems cut onions make people cry.

I am different from others, it is clear to see,
But that gives people choices of what we can be
And helps us answer the question "who am I?"

Suddenly, this beautiful girl was beside me.
She said that my cut was pretty nasty.
Her acceptance of me, made me teary eyed.

We are not the same at all in any way,
Yet we are still such good friends to this day
Because she gave a `cut up` onion a try.

Rejection hurts very much, to say the least
Whereas, acceptance creates so much peace.
It opens the doors to love, so don't let it pass you by.

BRAVE
light feeling

to face with courage and strength

SCARED
heavy feeling

to be frightened, to be fearful

At recess, at the slide, I was the first in line.
It was finally my turn to shine,
But then the playground got quiet – not one hooray.

I turned around in time to see
This bully named George Dupree.
He pushed in front and I bravely said, " HEY!"

He turned to me and raised his fist to punch.
I was shocked and almost lost my lunch.
I thought, " Oh my, on the ground I'm going to lay!"

But, instead of being scared and a coward
I suddenly became brave and empowered
And said, "That bullying won't work here, not today."

In shock, he just looked straight at me,
Maybe because a talking onion is a sight to see.
He just scratched his head, nodded and walked away.

It is not that being scared is bad.
If you don't feel brave, don't feel sad.
You are brave inside, no matter what people say.

CALM
light feeling

to be quiet, to be peaceful

FRUSTRATED
heavy feeling

to be irritated, to be annoyed

I was called up in front of my class
To explain a project I made out of glass,
But it is hard for me to say what I intend

Every time I get in front of a group
I turn into blended onion soup,
My words don't come to my mouth to send.

When I got home, I was so frustrated
My brain was totally deactivated
My Mom said, "Calm down and you will mend."

She said, "When we are frustrated, our minds race
We waste a lot of energy in the chase."
She gave me a solution on which I now depend.

She said, "Staying calm brings certainty to the mind,
Then our words just appear when we're in a bind.
They come to us just like an old faithful friend."

Oh for sure, challenges will still come.
Keep calm though, and don't go numb.
It worked for me so it's something I highly recommend.

DETERMINED
light feeling

to be firm, to not give up

DOUBTFUL
heavy feeling

to not trust, to be hesitant

I am not very good at cleaning my room.
I was born in a dirt garden, just before noon.
The idea of cleaning makes me want to scream.

One day, my friend stiffly said to me
Cleaning house was as easy as can be.
It really cut through my self esteem.

So the next day I was determined to try
To clean the kitchen after Chinese stir fry
But after five minutes, I lost all of my steam.

My doubt overcame me, I was crying on the floor
When my Mom walked through the door.
My failure seemed just so extreme.

She said, "Don't be doubtful, just keep going
Through determination, the results will start showing.
Believe me, it is not as bad as it seems."

I got determined, put on the music – this was my chance.
Not doubtful, I got out the broom and started to dance.
Suddenly, the kitchen was spotless – I had achieved my dream.

Energetic

Tired

ENERGETIC
light feeling

to be firm, to not give up

TIRED
heavy feeling

to not trust, to be hesitant

One morning at school, my teacher read this story
About an elephant caught in the lavatory.
While she read, the other kids did not say a peep.

When she finished reading, she asked us to pretend
Like we were stuck in the very same bend.
Wow, right out of my chair did I leap.

Suddenly, I realized I was the only one
Who was energetic and having so much fun.
The class laughed at me, which I thought was pretty cheap.

I felt embarrassed about being myself
I put the rest of my excitement on the shelf.
Soon I was tired and started counting sheep.

I went home crying, my Dad softly said to me,
"You are energetically unique as can be.
Stay true to yourself is advice I'd like you to keep.

You are meant to stand out, don't try to fit in.
Honor your energetic nature, it's your real origin.
By expressing your heart, you won't get tired and fall asleep."

FREE
light feeling

to be limitless, to be in peace

BURDENED
heavy feeling

to be troubled, to be weighed down

One day my friends and I cut through the neighbor's yard
It makes the walk home from school half as hard.
But there was my neighbor, furiously mad, it was unreal.

She yelled at me, "You are destroying my grass.
Didn't you know it is illegal to trespass?"
She was so close, I could smell her breakfast – it was oatmeal.

My Dad always told me that when you are in a fight
Keep your heart free and you will know what is right.
It is a burden not knowing if what we feel is real.

At that very moment, I just knew
That the very best thing I could do
Was agree that I was wrong in this ordeal.

She became free of her fury, it began to melt.
She could not stay frozen in how she felt.
My decision in this matter was obviously ideal.

It is a burden to feel like our choices are few.
We end up reacting instead of seeing it through.
Our greatest freedom is that we can change how we feel.

GIVING
light feeling

to be generous, to care about others

SELFISH
heavy feeling

to stingily keep things, to be not caring about others

I had my eye on this expensive toy.
I was sure it would be the height of all my joy.
Every chance, to my parents, I would drop a clue.

I did not care at all about the cost
The value of things got completely lost.
I selfishly did not consider my parent's revenue.

My Dad was mad. He loaded the car with my old toys
And took me to a homeless shelter for girls and boys;
A place of safety for when they need rescue.

He wanted me to make the donation
And give away my past toy accumulation
This stop was meant for me to take review.

What I saw made me feel so very sad
And reminded me to be giving with what I had.
I cried a lot and used up a whole box of tissue.

Sometimes, we all get selfish, I believe
We forget that when we give, we receive.
Receiving is great but giving is greater – believe me, it's true!

HAPPY
light feeling

to be cheerful, to be joyful, to be pleased

SAD
heavy feeling

to be gloomy, to be sorrowful

I had a fabulous dog named PicaBoo.
He was my best friend, we stuck together like glue.
Everywhere I went, he was sure to follow.

One day last year, he died and left the world.
Oh how my sadness just swirled and twirled.
I could not find any happiness, I felt so hollow.

Some of my friends said I had become a real downer
Because I was always a permanent frowner.
I just could not get over feeling sad and mellow.

One day my Mom said she knew I missed my friend
And she also felt our love would never end.
Then she opened the door and in came our new dog Yellow.

Yellow brings me so much joy, he made a difference
Sure, I still feel sad and miss PicaBoo since,
But my happiness returned and it's not shallow.

Feelings move and feelings change.
They are not set in stone – they rearrange.
A happier tomorrow is a great belief to swallow.

INSPIRED
light feeling

to be excited, to be delighted

DEPRESSED
heavy feeling

to be sad, to be disheartened

I tried out for the soccer team at school.
Inspired, I thought it would be pretty cool.
As an onion, I could roll with the ball continuously.

A depressing thing happened, I didn't make the cut.
I began acting out and got in a serious rut.
I was mad and started behaving obnoxiously.

When the season started, depression hit me hard.
I was quickly in a spiral, heading downward.
Sleep was the only activity I took on seriously.

My Mom said, "The way out of depression is to get inspired,
To serve others and find people you admire.
Focusing only on yourself, will keep you down, obviously."

Finally, I decided to go and see the coach
Since I could not play, I'd try a different approach.
To my shock, he needed an assistant, and I said "Definitely".

From this, I learned to make every obstacle an opportunity.
There is a gift in it that sometimes we simply cannot see.
Keeping inspired though is what makes dreams a possibility.

JOYFUL
light feeling

J

to be happy, to be carefree

HORRIBLE
heavy feeling

to be sad, to feel awful

It all began at practice for school choir.
We were singing about water and fire.
I was chosen to be the soloist for the concert in May.

When I sing, I feel my insides smile.
My joy is visible for many a mile.
I'd like to be Onionhead® the rock star someday.

But when my friends laughed at me, I felt like a misfit.
Horribly, my best friend Suzan took it to the limit.
I could not believe our friendship she'd betray.

Sadly, there was no time to even rejoice
For the next day I woke up without a voice.
I could not send my horrible feelings away.

That evening, there was a knock at my door
It was Suzan, she was staring at the floor.
She said, "I'm sorry I was so horrible yesterday."

I forgave her because I could tell she really cared
And knew my joy was something I wanted shared.
I made a promise to myself, my singing was here to stay.

KIND
light feeling

to be gentle, to be caring

MEAN
heavy feeling

to be nasty, to be cruel

One day, I was on the school bus.
In the back, there was a huge fuss.
A kid was being mean to this boy Rick hurtfully.

As I walked to my class, I started to think
That my behavior pretty much stinks.
I did not help so I was no kinder than the mean bully.

I did nothing, witnessing something wrong
So from him, I cannot sing a different song.
I was not kind and acted so unconsciously.

I went to Rick that day and we turned it around
Quickly, a beautiful new friendship was found.
But the trip home was still looming anxiously.

We agreed that if he got picked on, we'd stick together.
We'd show the bully kindness and try to make it better.
We won, because the two of us took it on to our capacity.

I think when we get mean, we go a little blind.
We get frightened and forget to be kind.
But kindness is what makes mean behavior end differently.

LOVE
light feeling

deep caring, strong affection

HATE
heavy feeling

to dislike greatly, to despise

For a while I was frequenting this word hate.
I hated strawberries, olives and dates.
The word hate in my world was getting energized.

One day I was playing with my best friend Roy
We fought and in the end he broke my toy.
I said, "I hate you" and he said, "You, I despise."

Words can carry a real hard punch.
It is how love ends up getting scrunched.
If words were hits, we'd both end up hospitalized.

I spoke to my Dad and he set me straight
About this issue of love and hate.
He felt my behavior had not been too wise.

He said, "That hate comes from anger or fear.
Hate has one want – for love to disappear.
That from my vocabulary, I should have it exorcised."

Every time we think or say the word hate
We are withholding love from its true fate,
So I went to all I had wronged and lovingly apologized.

MAGICAL
light feeling

to be wondrous, to be delightful

ASHAMED
heavy feeling

to be embarrassed, to be humiliated

One day I purposely stepped on a bug
I was ashamed, but I put it under the rug.
No one would know but the dead bug and me.

The next day when asked a question, I lied.
To this ashamed business, I was getting tied.
I thought I better get help to set myself free.

So I went to my Mom and told her what I did.
She said, "On these bad habits, put a lid."
I immediately answered, "I totally agree!"

She said, "Life is magical and all can be seen
No matter what you say or where you have been.
There are always angels to give us the key.

Our actions are watched because they care
To guide us to do what is always fair.
So ashamed of ourselves we will never be."

It is not that I won't make a mistake again
But I will try to be a good man amongst men.
Now I magically look up for a guardian angel to see.

NICE
light feeling

to be pleasant, to be polite

NASTY
heavy feeling

to be mean, to be spiteful

My Cousin Lula has an interesting personality.
She has a habit of constantly being nasty.
Her behavior was creating a pretty bad trend.

I decided to be nice when she asked me to race.
She tripped me and pushed ahead to first place.
Even though she cheated, her victory she would defend.

I was angry and frustrated, needless to suffice,
I said, " Truthfully, for your nastiness there is a price.
Is this why you do not have a single friend?"

When you are nasty, love is what you sacrifice
It is much better to be cooperative and nice.
Otherwise you will have no one on whom you can depend.

She looked at me confused like I was from outer space.
Then she suddenly understood and gave me an embrace.
And for all her nastiness, she nicely made her amends.

It was such an amazing, incredible victory;
She changed her nasty habit and listened to me.
It is wonderful to see niceness actually win in the end.

Outgoing

Lonely

OUTGOING
light feeling

to be friendly, to be sociable

LONELY
heavy feeling

to be cut off, to feel alone

My parents said we were moving to this mountain town.
Onions aren't meant for the snow belt, I frowned.
I felt this was a mistake of terrible extreme.

I went to my new school, kids laughed and stared.
One asked me if I bathed in non stick cookware.
This move was awful, I missed my onionized team.

I cried, I was lonely, I needed to make friends.
I'd have to get brave and risk being rejected again.
I gave myself a pep talk to raise my self esteem.

I was tired of feeling alone and wanted a new start.
I practiced saying hello, making `outgoing` a form of art.
I was ready to allow my light to brightly beam.

The next day I said hello to absolutely everyone.
I was myself again and people noticed I was fun.
Thank goodness my outgoing ways I could redeem.

We have to tell loneliness to get out of our way.
We have to be outgoing creating what we want each day.
This is the answer to making life a fun loving dream.

PEACEFUL
light feeling

to feel tranquil, to feel serene

MAD
heavy feeling

to be angry, to be agitated

I have a bad habit of always being late.
Even though I know it's bad to make people wait.
But I kind of thought - "What's the big deal?"

One morning because I was late, I missed the school bus.
My Mom had an appointment, so it was a big fuss.
She was mad – a feeling she did not want to conceal.

She said, "When you get home, we will need to talk.
Next time you miss the bus, you will have to walk."
I knew this was not the best time to make an appeal.

Would you believe my teacher's lesson was about time?
It was then I understood my Mom's anger and my crime.
He said we all depended on each other like spokes on a wheel.

My Mom kept her peace because her temper she never lost.
She never boiled over and never turned to frost.
She said she was mad, but she stayed peacefully genteel.

We all need to learn to respond to anger and not to react.
Face our feelings truthfully and keep our peace in tact.
If we all did this, the world would certainly heal.

QUIET
light feeling

to be in a state of calm, to speak softly

LOUD
heavy feeling

to be showy, to be noisy

Once on a hike, I was loud, talking indiscreetly
A butterfly landed on my arm, I missed it completely.
My Dad said, "You did not understand the butterfly show."

He said, "It is when we are quiet that we can reconnect
To a feeling of peace that is just so perfect.
It is then our seeds of wisdom can be sowed."

I didn't get it so I kept talking proudly.
I continued asking questions ever so loudly.
When my Dad asked if some quiet time he could borrow.

After ten minutes of silence, because I did obey
He said, "Quiet time lets your worries wash away."
So now I practice this method and go with the flow.

Because I learned to be quiet, I am now able to see
So many amazing things, I am even more aware of me.
I can now sit quietly which helps me to mindfully grow.

I have to be honest, I still talk and play in a loud way
I always ask a million questions each and every day.
But I also learned how to be quiet – it's a good thing to know.

RELAXED
light feeling

to be untroubled, to be at ease

STRESSED
heavy feeling

to be tense, to be worried

Let's face it, everyone has stress these days.
Sports, school, friends – worry comes in many ways.
We have to find a relaxing way to handle this issue.

As you can imagine, as an onion, I am not tall
But I badly wanted to play basketball.
I am short and wide, I know – not much value.

We had to line up, it was time for the teams to be chosen.
I was so stressed. I was sweating, yet I was frozen.
I was sure I'd be last picked....guess what?.... it was true!

At that moment there was a great thought I had,
"I may never play NBA, but for an onion, I'm not that bad.
I will just enjoy my teammates and keep my point of view."

All of a sudden, this relief came over me. I was so relaxed.
I was at peace with the world and not in the least bit taxed.
I would just give it my best shot and probably even make a few.

We all know that stress is something we can do without
But it comes with life and its lessons, so let's not pout.
Staying relaxed with it all, is the best avenue.

SAFE
light feeling

to be protected, to be relaxed

NERVOUS
heavy feeling

to be anxious, to be uneasy

It was my birthday and my family went outside.
They got me a new bike, I was beaming with pride.
I was about to jump on but my Mom made me delay.

She was nervous, thinking this was a bad call.
She made me wear pads thinking the bike was too tall.
You realize, an onion on a bike is quite a display.

My Dad was excited and ran behind me.
To be sure I was safe, he needed to see.
When he let go, I thought I would fly away.

Around the corner, I took a fall.
It helped so much that I'm a round ball.
I was shaken, but in the end, I was okay.

Everything I needed to be safe I had;
Head gear, back gear and many a pad.
I never got hurt, so my confidence didn't sway.

I got back on my bike and off I went.
'Love is safety', was the lesson sent.
I am ever so grateful for my parents to this day.

THANKFUL
light feeling

to be grateful, to be appreciative

UNGRATEFUL
heavy feeling

to be unappreciative, to not be thankful

I went on a treasure hunt at my Uncle Rob's house.
We had to find clues supposedly left by a mouse.
Whatever we found, we were to get a little money.

At one point my cousin wanted to quit.
She did not understand the fun we all got from it.
She was ungrateful and became quite whiney.

Oh, she made me overwhelmingly mad.
She was so horrible, it was really bad.
She never said thank you and behaved ungratefully.

I am the youngest of this onion bunch.
But I won because I had a strong hunch.
I so appreciated my Uncle Rob's creativity.

I was thankful to him because it was so great.
With his help from the game and my savings to date,
I was able to make a donation to my favorite charity.

I was happy to play seeing the joy it brought
And the money helped me to serve others a lot.
I was completely thankful for this sharing opportunity.

UNDERSTANDING
light feeling

to be sympathetic, to be supportive

INSENSITIVE
heavy feeling

to be unfeeling, to be uncaring

A kid in my school got hurt playing football.
It was really bad and he was in the hospital.
The whole school rallied around his family.

We had an assembly to get an update
To better understand about his difficult fate
When the girl I was next to laughed loudly.

I tried to let her insensitivity go,
I felt like she was a terrible foe.
But an understanding thought came to me.

Perfectly, later that day, I saw her again.
She was in a compromising situation.
While taking a test, she needed a pen desperately.

I helped her out, I did not say a thing.
She was so grateful for my understanding.
Her previous insensitivity left her feeling terribly.

Truths told, being insensitive is being cruel,
So listen carefully to the golden rule:
Understand others, as you'd like to be understood, ultimately.

VICTORIOUS
light feeling

to be triumphant, to win

DISAPPOINTED
heavy feeling

to be let down, to be sad

Because of my report card, my parents would be disappointed.
It was awful, my grades were not good and very disjointed.
I tried to think of a reason I could defend.

So I hid it where they would not find the spot.
I'd be disowned and have to live with Aunt Shallot.
The decision of hiding report cards, I don't recommend.

When I did give it to them, they read it line by line.
They only cared about what the teacher defined
About my efforts that I lazily did not extend.

My parents did not care about the grades I got;
It was my lack of effort that made them distraught.
But this disappointment, I could certainly mend.

Some teachers said I tried, some said I did not;
Only for not trying, in trouble I got.
It was a new definition of victory I could now comprehend.

If we try and fail, that is still victory and success
If we fail to try, we will be disappointingly less.
For it is only in the trying that we're triumphant in the end.

WILLING
light feeling

to be agreeable, to be cooperative

STUBBORN
heavy feeling

to be inflexible, to be immovable

People call me stubborn, yes it's true.
I correct them saying, "I'm very strong willed, thank you."
Willingness is something I strongly advise.

For the animal shelter, my Dad volunteered
They needed help with their building and he's an engineer.
He insisted I go, but I was mad and not energized.

When we got there, I tried stubbornly to make him wrong
But truth be told, it did not take very long
For incredible amounts of love to be realized.

The people at the shelter were so willing to let me help.
There were tons of puppies that squirmed and yelped.
I was thrilled and I sat there completely mesmerized.

When it was time to go, I did not want to leave;
I was willing to sleep there, if you'd believe!
To my Dad, I really needed to apologize.

Being stubborn is a complete waste of time.
Be smart, be willing, and open to serve on a dime.
When we say yes to life, unforgettable things actualize.

EXCITED
light feeling

to be eager, to be thrilled

BORED
heavy feeling

to be uninterested, to be uninspired

Truth be told, I get bored in the car.
I am constantly asking, "Okay, now how far?"
I complain a lot when my boredom is extreme.

My Mom tried to play a word game with me;
I was already lost in the land of boredom, you see.
When I am bored, time moves so slowly or so it seems.

I decided I would look into each car we passed by.
I wondered who they were, where they were going and why.
My wild thoughts and imagination, I began to redeem.

I opened my journal and started to write
About the exciting adventures that were taking flight.
My creativity was rushing through my bloodstream.

When we are bored, we can go to dark places.
We have to find excitement in other spaces.
When this happens, it's like staying on the team.

Feeling excited comes from being inspired.
Something just sparks us and our joy is on fire.
And before we know it, we create something supreme.

YUMMY
light feeling

to feel delicious, to feel delightful

YUCKY
heavy feeling

to feel disgusting, to feel uncomfortable

Since we moved to the mountains, my grandma lives far away.
I miss her because I use to see her every day.
Missing her felt yucky, a feeling I could not conceal.

One day I cried, I felt so very sad
I could not sleep, I felt so yucky and bad.
I called my grandma to help me resolve this ordeal.

Gram said, "Our yummy moments, live in your heart.
So you can always find me when we are apart.
On this you can always depend because it's very real."

After that, I could feel her touch my face;
I could smell her rose perfume and see her blouse of lace.
These moments definitely helped me to heal.

Whatever moments are yummy to you
Cherish and hold them to keep them true.
We'll need them for the times when life is not ideal.

I don't feel yucky anymore because in my heart, she is near.
I just know it because I can always feel her here.
I feel yummy that Gram and I are together in this deal.

ZESTFUL
light feeling

to be enthusiastic, to be dynamic

JEALOUS
heavy feeling

to be envious, wanting what others have

I have a friend, his name is Dan
When Dan does well, Dan is the man.
His big problem is that he has a jealousy issue.

If I got 100 on a test, he says he got 101.
If I won at a game, he'd ruin all the fun.
I wondered if our friendship should be continued.

For life, I have a natural zest.
Onions are different, but we're the healthiest.
Understanding the stink in others is our best virtue.

He resented my joy, one day he will have to learn
That his jealousy leaves others feeling a burn.
I hope he still has friends when he does this review.

We each have a long life ahead of us,
So we must make each moment happy and robust.
Jealousy is something where life loses it's value.

Having zest for life is being supportive of everyone,
Knowing that in their victories, we share in the fun.
Then our loving ourselves and others is right on cue.

needs Save the Rain

The *Onionhead*® family holds ourselves responsible for the health and well being for all of humanity.

In the developing world, a child dies every 15 seconds from lack of clean water. For these children, we have created our sister non profit called Save the Rain.

We teach communities in Africa to build rain catchment systems as a sustainable water supply, using only local materials and local work force. Our budget is $15.00 for a child to have clean water for the rest of their life and the lives of their offspring.

www.savetherain.org.

AMERICA
needs Onionhead®

In the way we believe the rain is the answer for the developing world, we believe the ability to handle our emotions intelligently is the answer for the developed world.

Life is 1% how we make it and 99% how we take it. Hidden in our deepest feelings is our highest truth. The more we accept and honor ourselves, the more we discover the miracle of our potential. One should never be ashamed of how they feel. Every emotion is understandable. It is what we do with them that counts.

The first seven years of a child's life are the most important. Therefore, the more we empower children to embrace life in a positive and constructive way, the better chance they will learn that choice, not chance, creates our destiny.

Onionhead® provides a direct and easy way to deal with feelings intelligently. We must approach life from a place of wellness rather than a place of wounds. It is said that as we teach, we learn. Our hope is that our little onion will enhance your life the way he has continuously enhanced ours.

...the beginning